CONTENTS

VOLCANO RESCUE

'We shouldn't be doing this, Jess. We're going to get into big trouble.'

'Look, Zac, my brother would be here by now if he could. Something's up. He would know before anyone else that the volcano is going to erupt today, with all the equipment he's got up there. If you don't want to help me rescue him, go back.'

'We're best friends,' says Ben.

'Yeah,' adds Amelie. 'Where you go, we go.'

'Sure,' says Zac quietly. 'But what's that funny smell?'

'Oh no,' Amelie shouts. 'It's sulphur **gas**. The volcano is going to blow sooner than they thought...'

'Nah, I can't see anything,' says Zac. 'It must be Ben's egg sandwiches that smell!'

WHAT DO YOU THINK?

Zac is right, there can't be a gas there if we can't see it.

OR

Amelie is right, gases exist and take up space even if we cannot see them.

PROVE IT!

Explore gases for yourself. You need:

- dry sponge
- bowl of water
- measuring jug

1 Squeeze the dry sponge very tightly to force the air out of the holes inside it. Keep squeezing.

2 Put the sponge in the bowl of water. Then let it go.

3 Lift out the sponge and quickly squeeze the water it contains into the measuring jug.

WHY IT WORKS

A sponge is made of a **solid** material, but has holes filled with air, a gas. You squeezed out the air and filled those spaces with water instead. By measuring how much **liquid** comes out of the sponge, you can work out how much gas was in there before! Amelie is right – gas can be there even if we can't see it.

EXPLOSION!

It feels eerily quiet and still on the hill as the friends climb higher. Suddenly there's a rustling sound from the trees, followed by a low growl and the crunching of twigs.

'Wh... Wh... What's that?' trembles Zac, reaching for Ben's arm.

'It's okay, Zac. It's just animals running from the slope,' Ben says. 'They can sense danger.'

'It's not okay. Look!' yells Jess, pointing to the top of the hill. 'The volcano is erupting!'

Clouds of smoke and something red and fiery are bursting out of the top of the volcano.

'That's lava,' shouts Amelie. 'It's burning hot liquid rock.'

'Don't be daft,' says Ben. 'Rock is hard and solid. It can't flow.'

WHAT DO YOU THINK?

Ben thinks solids can never be like liquids and flow.

Amelie says solids can become liquids when heated to the right **temperature**. This is called **melting**.

Who do you think is right?

PROVE IT!

You can test this idea, using chocolate instead of rocks!

You need:

- chocolate chips
- sealable plastic bag
- bowl of hot water
- paper plate

1 Put the chocolate chips into the bag and seal it tightly.

2 Hold the bag with the chocolate chips inside it in the bowl of hot water.

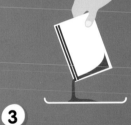

3 When the chocolate melts, take out the bag and open it. Pour the liquid chocolate onto the plate. Then put it in a cool place. What happens?

WHY IT WORKS

Heating chocolate changes it from a hard solid into a runny liquid. When liquids are cooled down enough, they can become solids. That's what happens when you put the melted chocolate in a cool place. Chocolate melts at quite a low temperature, but rock melts at a much higher temperature – such as you would find in the incredibly hot centre of the Earth. So Amelie is right again!

LAVA ON THE MOVE

The sky darkens and the air feels dangerously hot. Fiery hot lava is starting to roll down the sides of the mountain, burning trees and plants in its path.

'That's it,' shouts Zac. 'We have to turn back. Now!'

'No,' says Jess. 'I'm going on.'

'That lava is going to flow over this path any minute. Let's go the other way,' Ben pleads.

'That'll take too long,' yells Jess angrily.

'It's OK,' Amelie says. 'That lava looks thick and slow-moving. If we move fast, we should have time to get past the point where it's heading...'

WHAT DO YOU THINK?

Ben is right, liquids always flow quickly.

OR

Amelie is right, some liquids flow more slowly than others.

PROVE IT!

You can test this idea by racing liquids!

You need:

- four very small glasses or bottle lids
- funnel ● milk ● ketchup ● orange juice
- cooking oil ● large flat plastic chopping board
- tray ● watch with a second hand or a stopwatch

1

Use the funnel to fill one glass with milk, one with ketchup, one with oil and one with orange juice. Make sure they are all filled to the same level.

2

Lean the board against a chair to prop it up. Rest it on a tray to catch any mess! Now pour one glass of liquid at the top of the board. Ask a friend to record how long it takes to trickle down the board. Which liquid flows fastest?

WHY IT WORKS

Amelie is right. Liquids flow at different speeds. Liquids that are very **viscous**, such as oil and ketchup, are thick so they flow slowly. Liquids that are less viscous, such as milk, are thin and runny and they flow quickly. That's why thick lava tends to flow more slowly than thin, runny lava.

POISONED WATER

'I've got to stop for a minute. We're past that lava flow now, aren't we?' asks Zac nervously.

The friends rest by a stream to catch their breath. The air is getting hotter and feels very dusty and dry.

'I need a drink, but this water is full of bits of dust and ash,' sighs Amelie, looking at the water she's scooped into a cup.

Ben gets a clean hankie out of his rucksack and pours water through it to **filter** out the dirt.

'There you go,' he says proudly as he hands the cup to Amelie.

'Don't!' yells Jess, jumping forward to push the cup away from Amelie. 'There could be something poisonous **dissolved** in it!'

WHAT DO YOU THINK?

Ben is right, filtering bits of dirt from the water makes it clean.

OR

Jess is right, some dirt that we cannot see might be dissolved in the water.

PROVE IT!

You can test which things can be filtered out of water and whether certain things cannot be.

You need:

- sugar ● rice ● pasta ● two jugs
- water ● colander ● sieve

1 Fill a jug with water then add equal amounts of sugar, rice and pasta and stir it all up.

2 Pour the mixture through the colander into the second jug. Remove the colander and the pasta it trapped. The water is still not clean. What to do now?

3 Pour the mixture through the sieve back into the first jug, to filter out the rice. Taste the water. What do you notice?

WHY IT WORKS

We can separate large solids from liquids by filtering them through a colander, and smaller solids through a tighter mesh such as a sieve. Some solids, such as sugar, dissolve in water to form a **solution**. Jess is right: they break into pieces so tiny we cannot see them or filter them out.

PERILOUS PUDDLES

The roaring sound of lava setting fire to trees in the distance fills the air. The friends run quickly along, but heavy branches hanging over their path make it harder to see.

'I'm scared,' Amelie whispers to Jess.

'It's OK,' Jess replies. 'It's not far now.'

Suddenly, just ahead of them, they hear Zac scream and see him pulling Ben roughly backwards by his rucksack.

'Watch it!' warns Zac. 'There's **steam** coming from that puddle. If you step in it, it'll burn you.'

'You're slowing us down,' says Ben angrily. 'It's just dust and smoke from the volcano.'

'No', says Amelie. 'Zac's right. That water is **evaporating** and it must be VERY hot if it's making steam!'

?

WHAT DO YOU THINK?

Are Zac and Amelie right?
Does heat cause water
to evaporate?

PROVE IT!

You can test this idea.
You need:

- two zip-lock freezer bags ● cup ● water ● teaspoon
- two coloured paper towels

1 Put one cup of room-temperature water in one zip-lock bag, and seal it.

2 Ask an adult to help you carefully put one cup of very hot tap water into the other zip-lock bag, and seal it.

3 Put one paper towel on top of each bag. Put a drop of water in the middle of each towel. What happens to the drops of water?

WHY IT WORKS

When liquid water is heated gently, it turns into **water vapour**, an invisible gas in the air. This is called evaporation. The drop of water on the towel on the hot zip-lock bag disappears first because evaporation happens faster at higher temperatures. Steam occurs when water evaporates from boiling hot water, which is why we usually see it just above the spout of a boiling kettle. Zac and Amelie are right.

LIVES AT RISK

'This path is dangerous,' complains Zac, as the friends walk along a narrow path that skirts the edge of the slope. Just then, Amelie stumbles and falls. 'Noooo!' shouts Jess.

'Its OK – she's fallen onto a ledge just below us,' says Ben, finding a rope in his rucksack to haul Amelie to safety.

'Wait, stop pulling!' calls Amelie excitedly. 'There are diamonds sparkling inside the rock here – it's treasure!'

'There's no time. You're putting us all in danger,' yells Zac.

'Anyway, they're not diamonds,' snaps Jess. 'My brother says all sorts of **crystals** form when lava or liquid rock under the ground cools and hardens into **igneous rock**. Get moving!'

PROVE IT!

You can test this idea by making your own crystals.

You need:

- pipe cleaners ● cup
- tablespoon ● pencil
- string ● pyrex or ovenproof wide-mouthed jug or jar
- boiling water (ask an adult to help with this)
- borax from a supermarket (ask an adult to help with this too, and don't get it in your eyes)

1 Cut and twist the pipe cleaners into a shape that fits inside the jar without touching the sides or the bottom.

2 Ask an adult to fill the jar with cups of boiling water. Then put in three tablespoons of borax for every cup of water in the jar. Stir until it dissolves.

3 Tie the pipe cleaner to the centre of a pencil with string. Rest the pencil over the mouth of the jar so the pipe cleaner hangs in the borax water. Leave overnight. What happens?

16

? WHAT DO YOU THINK?

Jess says crystals can form from liquids. Can this happen? How?

WHY IT WORKS

Crystals can form when a liquid with lots of dissolved minerals in it cools down. Borax is a mineral that grows into crystals. Crystals can form in nature when melted rocks inside the Earth and on the Earth's surface cool and harden. Jess is right!

A DEADLY CROSSING

'There's my brother's research station, but it's been crushed by falling trees! Dan could be trapped inside,' shouts Jess, her eyes filling with tears. 'Move faster!'

'No – look!' trembles Zac. Just ahead of them is a narrow metal bridge. A deadly stream of red-hot lava bubbles threateningly from the gully below it.

'Heat from the lava will make that metal bridge boiling hot. We can't go that way,' says Amelie firmly.

WHAT DO YOU THINK?

Is Amelie right? Does metal **conduct** heat very easily?

PROVE IT!

You can test which materials conduct heat better than others.

You need:

- pan or big mug of very hot tap water
- three spoons: one metal, one plastic and one wooden, all the same size
- butter from the fridge
- three identical beads or small buttons

1 Take the three spoons and stick a bead to the end of each, using equal-sized blobs of very cold butter from the fridge. Each bead should be at the same height on each spoon.

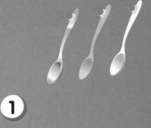

2 Put the three spoons into the pan or mug of very hot water. Which button falls off first? Which button falls off last?

WHY IT WORKS

Heat moves through solids by conduction. Some materials conduct heat better than others. Amelie is right. Metals conduct heat quickly. Some materials, such as plastic and wood, do not conduct heat well. These are called **insulators**.

'I've got it!' shouts Ben, excitedly. 'We can use this old wooden plank as a bridge.'

'No way,' argues Zac.'I can't walk over that. I'll get dizzy and fall. I'll risk the metal one.'

'There's no choice,' says Jess. 'The metal one will burn you. I'll help you across the plank. Come on!'

CHASED BY FLAMES

The friends find Dan, trapped under a fallen branch behind the crushed research centre. Together, they hurriedly lift the branch off Dan's leg to free him. With the roar of burning trees closing in on them, they race to Dan's truck on the path below.

'What's he doing?' demands Zac, watching Dan hurriedly wipe the windscreen. 'We have to go!'

'His wipers don't work. He's got to clear the windscreen first,' replies Jess.

'Won't it just blow clear as we go?' asks Ben. 'The flames are getting closer.'

'No,' says Amelie. 'It's **condensation**. When hot air hits the windscreen, the water vapour in it cools and turns back into water. The ash is sticking to the damp glass. We'll crash if we can't see where we're going!'

WHAT DO YOU THINK?

Is Amelie right that water vapour may turn back to liquid water when it cools?

PROVE IT!

You can test this idea with some simple equipment:

You need:

- large bowl
- hot water
- cling film
- bag of ice cubes
- small bowl or mug

1

Pour hot water into the large bowl and sit the small bowl carefully in the middle of it.

2
Cover the large bowl tightly with cling film.

3
Put the bag of ice cubes on the centre of the cling film. What happens?

WHY IT WORKS

The hot water evaporates and turns into water vapour. When this cools on the cold cling film, it turns back into water that drips into the small bowl. This is condensation. In the **water cycle**, water from the Earth's surface evaporates, condenses into clouds in the sky and falls back to Earth as rain. So Amelie is right again!

CRASH!

Speeding away from the flaming forest, Dan swerves to avoid a giant boulder thrown onto the road by the volcano. There is a loud 'pop' as one of the tyres bursts, and the truck skids into a ploughed field. While Dan rushes to change the tyre, the friends notice something strange on the ground.

'What's this?' asks Jess, pointing to a stone that looks like a giant snail.

'It must be something thrown up by the volcano,' says Zac.

'It's a **fossil**, the remains of a creature that lived here millions of years ago,' explains Amelie.

'But how come it's made of rock? How did it get here?' asks Ben.

? WHAT DO YOU THINK?

Is Amelie right? Can we see the shapes of animals formed in rock?

PROVE IT!

You can show how the shape of animals could form fossils.

You need:

- old candle ● small plastic tub
- sand ● water

1

Put a layer of sand into the bottom of the tub and pour enough water on it to make it damp. Push the shell into the wet sand to make a clear print in the sand when you remove it.

WHY IT WORKS

Amelie is right. Some fossils form when dead animals and plants are buried under mud and sand and slowly turn to rock with the natural materials around them. Some fossils happen when a shape, such as a footprint, presses into mud and fills with natural materials that harden into **sedimentary rock**.

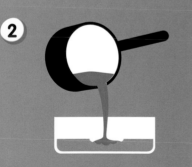

2

Ask an adult to melt the candle and pour hot wax into the shell shape in the sand.

3

When the wax is cold and solid, take it out of the sand. You should have a perfect 'fossil' of the shell!

RACING TO SAFETY

'I've fixed the tyre, get back in the truck right now!' Dan yells.

The friends leap in and the truck races down the slope towards safety. Looking out of the back of the vehicle, they see terrible scenes of destruction behind them. Smoke from burning trees is turning the sky black. Rocks tossed into the air by the eruption crash down nearby. Lava spills down the slope like deadly, bubbling treacle.

'Whoah!' says Zac. 'How did this happen?'

'Hot liquid rock from the Earth's centre forces its way up and suddenly bursts through the surface,' explains Dan. 'To thank you for rescuing me, I'll show you how to make a volcano at home, when we've recovered from all this excitement!'

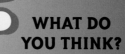

?

WHAT DO YOU THINK?

Is Dan right, can you create a volcano at home?

PROVE IT!

You can build a volcano of your own!

You need:

- jug ● vinegar ● tray ● red food colouring
- teaspoon ● plastic bottle with narrow top (no lid)
- funnel ● baking soda ● washing-up liquid

1 Add a couple of drops of red food colouring to the vinegar, and stir. This will make your lava red.

2 Stand the bottle on the tray. Use the funnel to put three full teaspoons of baking soda and a little washing-up liquid into the bottle.

3 Pour some of the coloured vinegar into the bottle and watch what happens next!

WHY IT WORKS

When liquid vinegar is poured onto solid baking soda, the chemicals **react** together to produce carbon dioxide gas that makes the mixture fizz up out of the bottle. Water can change from liquid to water vapour and back again, but this change to the vinegar and baking soda is **irreversible**.

QUIZ

1 Which of the following describes a solid, which describes a liquid and which describes a gas?

a) runny and takes the shape of the container you put it in

b) usually invisible and spreads all around to fill the space it is in

c) has a definite shape and doesn't pour or spread out

2 To change a solid into a liquid, would you

a) heat it?

b) bend it?

c) cool it?

3 When a solid dissolves in a liquid, what happens to it? Does it...

a) become a gas?

b) pass through a device to remove unwanted material?

c) break into pieces so tiny that we cannot see them?

4 Which of these three types of liquid has the highest viscosity?

a) milk

b) ketchup

c) water

5 To evaporate a liquid and change it into a gas, would you

a) cool it?

b) heat it?

c) filter it?

6 Can crystals form from...

a) liquids?

b) solids?

c) gases?

8 b | 9 b | 10 a | 11 a) igneous b) sedimentary | 12 b

7 **What is the word for the way heat moves through a solid?**

a) evaporation

b) conduction

c) insulation

8 **What is an insulator?**

a) a material that heat moves through easily

b) a material that heat does not move through it easily

9 **What are fossils?**

a) types of sea creatures alive today

b) remains of plants and animals preserved in rock over millions of years

c) types of gas

10 **What is condensation?**

a) when a gas cools and changes into a liquid

b) when a liquid evaporates and turns into a gas

c) when a solid melts and becomes a liquid

11 **Which of these statements describes sedimentary rock and which describes igneous rock?**

a) rock formed when liquid rock cools and hardens

b) rock formed over millions of years from layers of materials pushed together

12 **What word describes a change of state that cannot be changed back again?**

a) reversible

b) irreversible

FIND OUT MORE

BOOKS

Do Try This At Home! Punk Science
Macmillan Childrens Books, 2010

Everything Volcanoes and Earthquakes: Earthshaking Photos, Facts, and Fun!
(National Geographic Kids), National Geographic Society, 2013

Materials (Essential Physical Science)
Louise and Richard Spilsbury, Raintree, 2014

Materials (Real Size Science)
Rebecca Rissman, Raintree, 2013

Material World: The Science of Matter (Big Bang Science Experiments)
Jay Hawkins, Windmill Books, 2013

Stuff! Materials and How They Change (Real Scientist)
Peter Riley, Franklin Watts, 2012

Volcano (Eye Wonder)
Dorling Kindersley, 2013

WEBSITES

Watch cartoons about solids, liquids and gases:
www.abpischools.org.uk/page/modules/solids-liquids-gases

Explore different materials, how they are processed and what they are used for:
www.museumnetworkuk.org/materials

Watch a series of videos about changing materials:
www.rsc.org/learn-chemistry/resource/res00000913/changing-materials-demonstrations

See a flash animation explaining how volcanoes work:
www.guardian.co.uk/flash/volcanoes.swf

GLOSSARY

condensation when water vapour in the air cools and changes into liquid

conduct how heat moves through a solid

crystal special three-dimensional solid with flat sides and a regular shape

dissolve when a solid seems to disappear into a liquid

evaporate to change from a liquid into a gas

filter to pass something through a mesh to remove unwanted material

fossil remains of a plant or animal preserved in rock over millions of years

gas gases have no definite shape and spread out to fill the entire space available

igneous rock rock formed when lava or underground liquid rock cools and hardens

insulator material that does not allow heat to move through it easily

irreversible impossible to change back

liquid liquids are runny and take the shape of the container they are in

melting what happens when a solid is heated and becomes a liquid

react when two or more substances come into contact with each other and change to produce one or more new substances

sedimentary rock rock formed over millions of years from layers of natural materials

solid solids have a definite shape and don't pour or spread out

solution liquid in which something has been dissolved

steam mixture of very hot invisible gas and tiny water droplets

viscous describes a liquid that is thick and slow-moving

water cycle the constant movement of water between Earth's oceans, atmosphere and land

water vapour invisible gas in the air, water in its gaseous form

INDEX

THE LAST TRAIN

KIM LEWIS

WALKER BOOKS
LONDON

On the old railway line stood a hut. Railway men used to have their tea there, when they worked on the line. But now the tracks were gone and the hut was empty.

That very hot summer, sheep used the hut. They rubbed their newly shorn fleeces against the walls and put their heads up the chimney to escape the flies. More and more gaps appeared in the walls. One day the door finally crashed to the ground.

Sara and James stopped on their bicycles to look.

"Let's make a camp," Sara said. She and James left their bicycles and clambered into the hut. They worked all morning, stuffing the cracks with wool and grass and stamping the dirt floor as flat as they could.

They leaned out of the window and dreamed of the last train running through their farm. They thought they could see it, huge and puffing, as it rushed swift and mighty past the old hut. They thought they could hear it, horn wailing and wheels clattering fast on the tracks. They imagined being railway workers and signalled to the driver as he sped by, high up in his cab.

But the wind blew through the gap where the door used
to be and the stuffing fell out of the cracks. The railway hut
looked much as it had before.

"Some camp," declared James. They sadly wheeled
their bicycles home.

Mum and Dad were busy in the sheep pens. They finished work to sit on the wall.

"The railway hut is going to fall down soon," sighed Sara, slumping beside them.

"Will you help us save it?" pleaded James.

It was very hot, but they still set out, with tools and bits of wood, string and old carpet, bales of hay, pots and pans, all balanced on James' go-cart.

Sheep gathered to watch, as the cart rumbled along the railway line to the hut.

Dad and James made a shutter for the window. Mum and Sara made a door. They used the hay bales for seats and laid bits of wood and old carpet on the floor. They worked all afternoon, forgetting about time.

"Look!" James shouted to the waiting sheep. "Look at Railway Cottage now!"

Sara pinned her red handkerchief up by the fireplace.

"Whoever waves this when they stand by Railway Cottage will see a train," she said, "and the driver will stop."

Mum and Dad looked at each other and smiled.

"Tell us all about trains," said James.
He and Sara snuggled up on the bales, as evening drew in, very still and close.

Dad, who remembered steam trains, talked about when he'd watched them as a boy. Mum said she'd seen a photo in the village shop of a steam train stopped at the old village station.

The hot day darkened and a hush seemed to hold the air. Suddenly a gust of wind blew open the shutter.

James scrambled up and
leaned out of the window.
Rain fell on his face.
A crack of lightning split the
hot air, just as low rumbles
swelled from the hills.

Quickly Sara grabbed the
red handkerchief and
flew out of Railway Cottage.

James froze. In a thundering hiss of steam, a train blew out of the wind, carrying a wreath on the front. He watched unbelieving, as the train grew bigger and bigger, puffing slower and slower, steam billowing out over the railway line. He saw Sara wave the red handkerchief. Rain hissed down on the hot train, spitting on the metal.

James raced out of Railway Cottage. He and Sara took turns waving the red handkerchief. They waved and waved. The train brakes thundered and squealed. The driver poked his head out of the brightly lit window, high up in his cab. He smiled and waved back.

"Thunderstorm!" shouted Mum and Dad,
stumbling out of Railway Cottage. Rain was falling
in slanting hard drops, faster and faster, pelting on
the tin roof of Railway Cottage. Mum grabbed
Sara and James' hands and pulled them along the
railway line, throwing jumpers over their heads.

In another flash of lightning,
Sara looked back. Railway Cottage
stood by itself, snug against the
rain, a last plume of smoke
curling out of the chimney.

But the railway line was empty
and the train was gone.

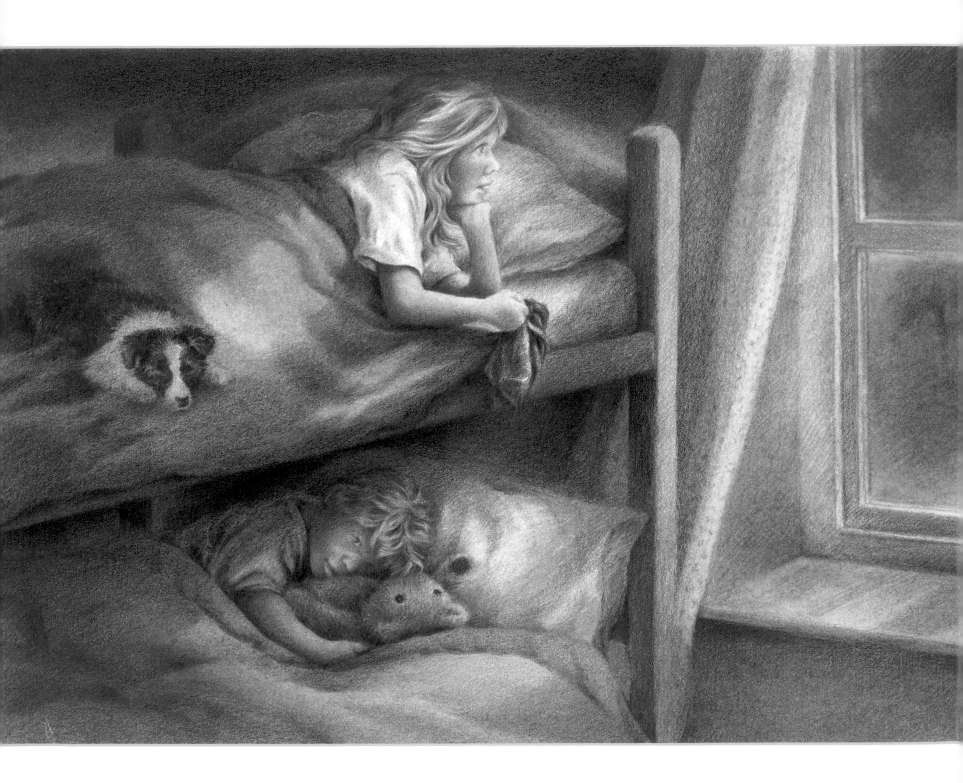

They shook the wet out of their clothes at home, shivering and laughing while it thundered and rained outside.

Mum and Dad tucked Sara and James into bed, but Sara could hardly sleep. She clutched the red handkerchief. James chattered excitedly, "We saw it! We saw the last train at Railway Cottage!"

Mum and Dad kissed them.

"Of course you did…" they said and smiled.

But Sara and James lay awake. They listened for trains in the rain, and whispered to each other in the dark.